T0383179

LESSONS LEARNED OVER THE PAST 50 YEARS
WITH COBURN SUPPLY COMPANY

ACCELERATE YOUR CAREER

IN THE

WHOLESALE DISTRIBUTION BUSINESS

ALFRED "TREY" BERLIN III

Accelerate Your Career in The Wholesale Distribution Business
Lessons Learned over the past 50 Years with Coburn Supply Company

©2023 Alfred "Trey" Berlin III

print ISBN: 979-8-35092-044-4
ebook ISBN: 979-8-35092-045-1

CONTENTS

CHAPTER 1:

RECRUITING YOUNG PEOPLE FOR THE DISTRIBUTION BUSINESS

In today's rapidly evolving world of technology, the distribution business is undergoing significant transformations. With the advent of the internet, email, and internal programs, many mundane physical tasks are being streamlined, reducing costs. However, to leverage these advancements effectively, we need to strengthen our workforce with entry-level employees who are eager to learn both traditional paper-based processes and the new technologies that accompany them. Currently, 80% of our staff is already adept at working with cutting-edge technology, and this percentage is expected to increase with proper training.

Tapping into an Untapped Market

Interestingly, a large number of job seekers currently overlook wholesale distribution as a potential career path. 50% of individuals looking for jobs have never even interviewed for a position in the distribution sector. This presents a unique opportunity for us to attract fresh talent and introduce them to the numerous career prospects our industry offers. From high school graduates and vocational-technical school attendees to community college graduates and those pursuing trades or various levels of college education, our industry provides a strong career path for individuals from diverse backgrounds.

The Enthusiasm of the 17-24 Age Group

Within the 17-24-year-old age group, there exists a notable eagerness to learn and explore the distribution business. These young individuals have a stronger desire to acquire knowledge and understand the intricacies of our industry. By nurturing their enthusiasm and providing them with the necessary training, we can shape a brighter future together.

The Power of Creativity and Lifelong Learning

To build a prosperous future, we must harness the power of innovative minds. There is nothing as futile as efficiently executing tasks that should not be done at all. It is these creative minds that will help us uncover new and more efficient ways of conducting business. Emphasizing that learning is a lifelong process, we encourage our workforce to stay abreast of industry changes and continuously seek personal and professional growth. Our most urgent task is to instill a love for learning and adaptability within our employees.

The Significance of Objectives and Effective Leadership

We believe in the effectiveness of management by objectives, provided we clearly define our goals. No business can solely rely on geniuses to manage its operations. Instead, we must build an organizational structure that enables average individuals to work together under competent leadership. This ensures the continuity and stability of our business.

The Continuous Need for New Talent

Recruitment should always be a priority for us. We should consistently seek out individuals who are eager to learn and contribute to our business. By maintaining a culture of learning and growth, we can attract motivated individuals who are enthusiastic about understanding and excelling in our industry.

Importance of Process Knowledge

To achieve operational excellence, everyone within our organization should possess a solid understanding of our key processes. This includes receiving, storing materials, and transferring goods, as well as the accounts receivable process. Sharing knowledge and promoting cross-functional expertise will strengthen our operations and improve overall efficiency.

Conclusion

In conclusion, the distribution business is evolving, and to stay ahead, we need to recruit young talent who are open to learning both the traditional and technological aspects of our industry. By tapping into the untapped market of job seekers and appealing to the enthusiasm of the 17-24 age group, we can shape a successful future. Encouraging creativity, lifelong learning, and effective leadership will ensure the sustained growth of our business. Let us continue to prioritize recruitment, foster a culture of learning, and empower our workforce with process knowledge to excel in the distribution industry.

CHAPTER 2:

NURTURING A STRONG ORGANIZATIONAL CULTURE

Culture serves as the secret ingredient that keeps employees motivated and customers satisfied. It permeates every aspect of our organization and becomes a way of life for our team members. From what they eat and wear to the way they walk, talk, treat death, and greet newborns, our culture shapes our collective identity and impacts our relationships with both internal and external stakeholders.

Sales Culture

In the realm of sales, responsiveness is key. The number one expectation of our customers is a salesperson who follows up promptly. Understanding the life cycle of a distributor, we know that it typically spans seven years. During the first two years, costs tend to be high as we establish relationships and build trust. Between years two and six, we experience the best growth opportunities. However, after the seven-year mark, the focus shifts primarily to price. It is crucial to adapt our sales approach accordingly.

Recognizing the changing dynamics, we acknowledge that the value of an outside salesperson diminishes as customers become acquainted with our inside sales force. As customers become satisfied and develop relationships with our inside team, the role of the outside salesperson transitions to acquiring new customers. Understanding this evolution is essential, as relying solely on outside sales would jeopardize our business.

Management Culture

In the world of the distribution business, measurement and evaluation are incredibly important. Dr. Mike Workman, a professor at TX A&M College of Industrial Distribution, emphasizes this crucial aspect. We firmly believe in measuring every part of our operations, knowing that around 40% of what we do may not be necessary.

When one of our key team members invests time in a commercial bid that we don't win, it's essential to conduct a review. We should reach out to the contractor who requested the bid and inquire about where we stood in terms of pricing. This helps us learn and improve. Keeping our best foot forward is a key principle.

As a manager, you should always be on the lookout for opportunities to enhance processes and increase efficiency.

If we take a closer look at our work, we'll realize that our primary task is to handle the movement of materials in and out. We allocate a significant portion of our budget to gaining new customers and making sales. In our line of business, continuous sales growth is crucial; without it, we cannot truly progress.

Discovering profits through pricing is an essential aspect of our operations. While many of our materials are priced according to market rates, our skilled sales team employs strategic margin calculations to set prices. Our ultimate goal is to maximize profits by leaving no money on the table. This skill comes with experience, and we recognize the value of mentorship for new salespeople. Pairing them with seasoned sales professionals who provide guidance and follow specific frameworks allows them to gain valuable experience over time. To gauge the effectiveness of management, we evaluate gross profit per full-time employee.

For example - An inside salesperson should be able to produce $18,000 gross profit per month. This is an easy way to measure your crew, some are at $12K, some at $18K, and some at $25K. You could have a star that is producing $25-30K per month.

Promoting a Culture of Excellence

At our company, we believe in doing things right from the start, as mistakes can lead to significant costs. For example, a simple delivery error may cost us $50 initially, but fixing it can add up to $150 more. That's why we put a strong emphasis on efficiency and accuracy, which helps protect our profits.

If, by any chance, something is missing from a delivery when it reaches the job site, it creates problems. We spend $50 to bring the order to the site, and then we need to spend an additional $100 on things like time, effort, and gas to fix the mistake. To address this, we keep track of each error and work on a plan to prevent them from happening again.

Our ultimate goal is to do everything right the first time, and we work hard to achieve that. Furthermore, I encourage striving for zero-error deliveries. Once we achieve this goal at our branch, we can proudly showcase it in our local marketing efforts, demonstrating our commitment to excellence and reliable service.

Controlling expenses is a fundamental aspect of bottom-line management, which is equally as crucial as driving sales or top-line management. This presents a challenge for managers who must simultaneously prioritize expense control and revenue growth. Balancing these two aspects requires diligence and strategic decision-making.

Conclusion:

Our organizational culture is the essence of who we are and how we operate. Nurturing a strong culture allows us to motivate our employees and provide exceptional service to our customers. By understanding the evolving nature of sales and adapting our approach accordingly, we can capitalize on growth opportunities. Emphasizing measurement, evaluation, and efficiency in management enables us to uncover hidden profits and control expenses. Cultivating a culture that values doing things right the first time ensures we remain profitable and successful. Let us continue to embrace and enhance our culture as we strive for excellence in all aspects of our business.

CHAPTER 3:

EFFICIENT OPERATIONS FOR SUCCESS

Introduction:

Smooth and efficient operations are the backbone of the organization. By implementing key strategies and focusing on continuous improvement, we can optimize the processes and enhance overall performance. This section highlights important considerations and actions that can contribute to our operational success.

Order Fulfillment:

To ensure exceptional service, it is crucial to staple ourselves to each order and meticulously follow every step of the process. This dedication allows us to maintain accuracy, timely delivery, and customer satisfaction.

Inventory Management:

Aiming for six turns on our inventory is an achievable goal, especially with the implementation of central warehouse replenishment. This approach enables us to optimize inventory levels, minimize carrying costs, and ensure product availability when needed. Additionally, a dedicated individual should handle returned goods to streamline the process and maintain consistency.

Product Line Limitation:

Limiting the number of similar product lines to two at each branch promotes efficiency and prevents excessive stock variation. This focused approach helps optimize inventory management and simplifies product handling.

Credit Management:

Monitoring and measuring the number of credits issued monthly provide valuable insights into our performance. By aiming to reduce credits, we emphasize the importance of getting it right the first time. This approach enhances customer satisfaction and indicates the effectiveness of our operations.

Effective Inventory Monitoring:

Maintaining the right inventory is vital for smooth operations. The Want List plays a crucial role in discovering items that are out of stock and alerts management to the need for new items. Regularly reviewing the CIR (Category Inventory Report) provides essential information on gross margin return for each product category, enabling us to make informed decisions about inventory management.

Diverse Product Offerings:

Customers value convenience and one-stop shopping experiences. Promoting our wide range of products, including Plumbing, AC, utilities, appliances, electrical, and more, can attract customers seeking comprehensive solutions. By highlighting our diverse offerings, we can enhance customer loyalty and satisfaction.

Special Orders and Returns:

Understanding the costs associated with special orders, small orders, and returns is essential for effective management. Designating an inventory manager for each region ensures accurate tracking, cost analysis, and efficient handling of these specific inventory situations.

Performance Measurement and Development:

Motivating employees, clear communication, performance measurement, and development are critical aspects of operations. Regularly measure performance through metrics such as the number of tickets processed daily using tools like Phocas. Encourage employee growth and provide development opportunities to foster a motivated and high-performing team.

Conclusion:

Optimizing our operations requires attention to detail, efficient processes, and continuous improvement. By closely monitoring order fulfillment, striving for optimal inventory turnover, managing credits effectively, and diversifying our product offerings, we can strengthen our operations. Tracking dead stock, managing special orders and returns, and measuring performance provide valuable insights for decision-making and improvement. By promoting employee motivation, communication, and development, we cultivate a high-performing team that drives our success. Let us prioritize efficient operations and continuous improvement as we strive to deliver excellence in all aspects of our business.

CHAPTER 4:

TRUE CULTURE

Culture is what keeps us motivated and makes our customers happy. It's not just about rules and values – it's a way of life for all of us.

In our culture, we understand that it's not only about the work we do or the things we sell but also about how we act and treat each other. Our culture influences the way we behave, our attitudes, and even the small choices we make every day.

One important part of our culture is the food we share. Whether it's team-building meals or snacks during breaks, eating together brings us closer and creates a friendly and inclusive environment where everyone feels valued.

Our clothing also reflects our culture. We dress professionally and take pride in our appearance, showing our customers that we take our responsibilities seriously and are dedicated to giving them the best experience.

But culture is more than just looks – it's about our actions. The way we walk, with confidence and purpose, shows our commitment to doing our best. It tells others that we're always ready to face challenges and achieve great results.

Good communication is another key aspect of our culture. The way we talk, both with our team and with customers, shows that we value clear and respectful communication. We listen actively, show empathy, and make sure everyone feels heard and respected.

Our culture extends beyond work to how we support each other in difficult times. We show compassion and care when someone experiences a loss. We create a supportive environment because we know that our success as a team depends on our genuine concern for one another.

We also celebrate new beginnings as part of our culture. When a baby is born, we show our happiness and appreciation for the joys of life. It strengthens the bond we share as a work family and reminds us to support each other in all stages of life.

To sum up, our culture is present in every aspect of our organization. It shapes how we eat, dress, walk, talk, and even how we handle difficult moments and celebrate new beginnings. By nurturing and preserving our culture, we create a positive work environment where employees feel motivated, customers feel satisfied, and success naturally follows.

CHAPTER 5:

ENCOURAGING STAFF PARTICIPATION

Encouraging staff participation is crucial in today's digital age, where the widespread availability of the Internet and email has significantly reduced communication costs. To shape a successful future, organizations must actively embrace innovation and create an environment where employees feel empowered to ask questions, even if it means admitting their ignorance. By fostering a culture that values curiosity and encourages staff to actively contribute their ideas and perspectives, organizations can tap into the collective intelligence and creativity of their workforce.

Effective time management is essential in maximizing productivity and achieving desired outcomes. Time is a finite resource, and without proper management, other tasks and responsibilities may suffer. By prioritizing tasks, setting clear goals, and utilizing techniques such as delegation and scheduling, individuals and organizations can make the most efficient use of their time, leading to improved performance and overall effectiveness.

Taking calculated risks is necessary for growth and innovation. Avoiding risks altogether often leads to missed opportunities and stagnation. While efficiency is valuable, it becomes meaningless if applied to tasks that are ultimately unnecessary. Organizations need to foster a culture that encourages calculated risk-taking, where employees feel empowered to explore new ideas, experiment, and learn from both successes and failures. By embracing a mindset that values innovation and entrepreneurial thinking, organizations can unlock new possibilities and drive meaningful change.

Recognizing that learning is a lifelong process is essential in a world of constant change. Organizations should prioritize ongoing education and professional development, both for individual employees and as a collective effort. Teaching others how to learn becomes a pressing task, as it enables individuals to adapt and acquire new skills in response to evolving challenges and technologies. By promoting continuous learning and providing resources and opportunities for growth, organizations can stay ahead of the curve and foster a workforce that is agile, adaptable, and ready to embrace new opportunities.

Innovation serves as a driving force behind entrepreneurship and the creation of new wealth. Organizations that actively encourage and support innovation can harness their resources and capabilities to develop new products, services, and processes that meet evolving market needs. By fostering a culture that rewards creativity, encourages risk-taking, and provides the necessary resources and support, organizations can fuel entrepreneurial spirit within their workforce and unlock untapped potential.

While "Management by Objectives" can be an effective approach, it requires a clear understanding of the objectives themselves. Sometimes, organizations may struggle with defining precise and measurable objectives, leading to misalignment and confusion. To ensure the success of management by objectives, organizations must invest time and effort into clearly articulating their goals, communicating them effectively to employees, and establishing a framework for monitoring progress and providing feedback.

The survival of any institution depends on its leadership. While exceptional talents can certainly make a difference, it is the collective effort of average individuals that sustains and propels an organization forward. Effective leadership is about empowering and inspiring individuals at all levels, fostering collaboration, and creating an inclusive and supportive environment where everyone can contribute their unique skills and perspectives. By recognizing and leveraging the strengths of their workforce, organizations can build a resilient and high-performing team capable of navigating challenges and driving success.

By embracing these principles and fostering a culture of continuous learning, adaptability, and innovation, organizations can thrive in an ever-changing landscape. By valuing employee participation, effective time management, calculated risk-taking, ongoing learning, and entrepreneurial thinking, organizations can unleash the full potential of their staff and position themselves for sustained success in the future.

CHAPTER 6:

UNDERSTANDING YOUR MARKET

Understanding your market is crucial for business success, comparable to choosing between an aisle seat or a window seat on a plane. Opting for the window seat grants you an opportunity to observe and comprehend the market landscape, enabling you to make informed decisions about where to invest your time, talent, and financial resources. It's akin to the experience of returning from an enlightening convention and, while flying back home, being able to visualize the potential for sales and strategically plan your next moves.

However, to effectively navigate the market, it is equally important to have a deep understanding of your own business. As renowned management expert Peter Drucker famously stated, the purpose of a business is to create a customer. This perspective emphasizes the fundamental importance of focusing on customer needs and delivering value that meets or exceeds their expectations.

Identifying indicators of a failing business is crucial for proactive management. Signals such as declining profit margins, escalating personnel costs, and simultaneous increases in sales volume can be warning signs that demand attention. As a manager, your primary objective is to take the lead, guiding and motivating your team towards success. By cultivating strong leadership skills, you can inspire your team members to perform at their best, adapt to changes in the market, and contribute to the growth and prosperity of the organization.

The second objective encompasses a range of critical elements that contribute to business growth and success. These elements include increasing revenues through strategic initiatives, defining and upholding high customer service standards, optimizing pricing strategies to enhance profitability, identifying opportunities to reduce the cost of serving customers without compromising quality, forging new customer relationships, improving gross margins by managing costs and enhancing efficiency, representing selected suppliers that align with the company's goals and values, and providing expertise in both product development and process improvement. These objectives collectively support the overall expansion and prosperity of the business, ensuring its long-term viability in a competitive marketplace.

By understanding the market dynamics, staying attuned to the needs and preferences of customers, and effectively managing your business with clear objectives in mind, you can position your organization for growth and success. Just as selecting the window seat on a plane offers a panoramic view of the world below, embracing these principles provides you with a broader perspective and strategic advantage in the ever-evolving business landscape.

CHAPTER 7:

3 CULTURES OF OUR BUSINESS

Within our business, we have three distinct cultures: sales, management, and operations. When we align two of these cultures, the third naturally follows suit, creating a harmonious and efficient organization.

In the realm of sales, we understand that the life cycle of a customer in our business typically spans around 7 years. The initial 0-2 years can be costly as we establish the relationship and meet their needs. The sweet spot for us lies in the 2-6 year range, where we can provide excellent service and build long-term loyalty. However, after 7 years, the customer's primary focus often shifts to price.

It's essential to recognize that the value of an outside salesperson diminishes as the customer becomes more familiar and comfortable with our inside sales team. To foster growth, information must flow efficiently to the customer through multiple inside sales people. The outside salespersons job is to go find new customers.

In the realm of management, we emphasize the importance of measuring every aspect of our operations. As Dr. Workman suggests, about 40% of what we do is unnecessary. Evaluating our team's activities and performance allows us to identify inefficiencies and address bottlenecks. Managers can gain valuable insights by working alongside different employees, understanding their challenges, and analyzing performance.

To be effective managers, we must also be well-informed about our competitors. It is essential to know the key customers of our competitors, especially the top 15, and develop relationships with their key employees. Sharing this information strategically within our organization helps us stay competitive and make informed business decisions.

We have all heard the saying, "Do it right the first time." This principle, originating from the military, underscores the importance of delivering quality and excellence in every interaction. While customers may grant us a second chance, we should strive to do it right every time, as multiple opportunities might not always be guaranteed.

Ultimately, the true test of management lies in our ability to generate profit. Amidst the myriad of tasks and responsibilities, profitability serves as the ultimate measure of success. Dr. Workman's observation that 40% of our actions are unnecessary further emphasizes the need to distinguish between urgent and important matters. This prioritization ensures that our efforts are focused on driving meaningful outcomes and maximizing our resources.

Control Expenses

Successful managers believe in assigning one person to handle returned goods and emphasize the importance of measuring the number of credits each month. Additionally, customers expect us to maintain accurate inventory quantities to facilitate convenient one-stop shopping.

Special Orders

Procuring special items and managing logistics, including freight and special charges, requires a trained specialist. This individual should also possess familiarity with the specific product being ordered.

Large Branch Specialist

Branches with a significant workforce, such as 30 employees, require specialists in various roles. Everyone must understand the processes related to receiving, storing, and shipping materials.

Finding the Right People

Continuously conducting interviews is essential since we always need new individuals who are eager to learn about our business. Tom Bromley with LCR later moved to Home Depot, told me that he never stops interviewing. When he finds good people, he saves their application and files them away, so that next time he is looking for new talent, he goes directly to his file first.

Correct Number of People

A metric to measure the monthly gross profit earned by each full-time employee (GP\$/FTE) is crucial. The target number can be determined by dividing the branch's gross profit by the number of full-time employees. When the answer becomes \$12,000 is the target.

Control Expenses and Grow Sales

Both controlling expenses and growing sales are essential for success. With the increase in the number of branches, it is now possible to monitor every expense category as a percentage of gross profit. People represent the largest expense category, and by employing budgeting and calculating percentages, we can effectively control expenses.

To-Do List

While acknowledging the availability of computerized systems, it is recommended that managers take a moment at the end of each day to create a to-do list for the following day. Unchecked items from the current day should be added. A prioritized list can significantly enhance productivity.

Low Margin Sales

Two types of low-margin sales exist. The first type involves large-volume sales with low margins, typically requiring discussions among managers, department heads, and salespeople before the sale. The second type comprises low-margin sales with regular quantities, which should raise concerns if they account for less than 23% margin.

Operations

Managers can derive great value by thoroughly understanding every process alongside operations personnel. It is beneficial to immerse oneself in the order or process, identifying potential bottlenecks and analyzing performance.

Inventory turnover plays a significant role. Generally, having 5-6 inventory turns is considered acceptable. The margin is another important factor to consider. Many distributors utilize the concept of "turn times earn," such as multiplying 6 turns by a margin of 0.25 to obtain a "Turn Earn" of 150. 150 Should be your goal.

Detailed reports can provide insights into turns, margins, and GMROI for each category.

The required number of product lines at a branch may vary based on its size. Some experienced individuals suggest that two lines of any product might be sufficient, but a thorough discussion within the branch can help determine the optimal approach.

Employees

Regular and structured employee reviews are essential for effective management. By conducting monthly reviews with inside sales employees, managers can gain valuable insights into their performance, identify areas for improvement, and provide timely feedback. Managers should meet with outside sales employees monthly to review assigned accounts with variance in sales and margin. For low-performing employees, additional training and coaching can be instrumental in helping them enhance their skills and capabilities, especially in areas such as "Selling Boldly" to boost sales and profitability. Setting clear performance goals is vital for order writers and inside sales personnel, aiming to generate over $18,000 in gross profit emphasizes the importance of driving revenue and maximizing profitability. These performance benchmarks serve as a guiding force, motivating employees to excel and contribute to the overall success of the company. Through consistent monitoring and support, managers can empower their team members to thrive and reach their full potential, ultimately contributing to the organization's growth and prosperity.

Inventory

The measurement of GMROI (gross margin return on inventory) is a valuable tool to assess inventory performance. The GMROI number indicates performance, such as a value of 130 for copper fittings. This means that if we invested $100 in copper fittings, we would receive a return of $130 at the end of the year.

Dead Stock refers to inventory that has not generated any sales within a year. The Inventory Specialist should prioritize selling or disposing of all Dead Stock. Dead stock costs the company between 1%-2% per month. It's important to have an ongoing plan to sell off Dead Stock. It's ultimately a cost to the branch.

Control Expenses

Knowing your market: Understanding the market allows you to identify where to invest your time, talent, and money. Similar to choosing between an aisle seat or a window seat on a plane, the window seat provides an opportunity to visualize the potential of sales when returning from an informative convention.

Knowing your business: The purpose of a business, as stated by Peter Drucker, is to create a customer. Predictors of a failing business include declining margins, increasing people costs, and increasing sales volume, all occurring simultaneously.

Manager's #1 objective: As a manager, your primary objective is to be a leader in your field, setting an example for others.

Manager's #2 objective: The secondary objectives may include increasing revenues, defining customer service standards, optimizing pricing strategies, decreasing the cost of serving customers, developing new customer relationships, increasing gross margins, representing chosen suppliers, and providing expertise in products and processes.

The 3 cultures in our business: The three cultures within the business are sales, management, and operations. Aligning two of these cultures will naturally influence the third to follow suit, creating a cohesive and unified environment.

In Sales: The most important thing a customer wants is an inside or outside salesperson who will follow through on their commitments and promises.

Return Goods: Many successful managers advocate for a designated person to handle returned goods. Additionally, it is advisable to measure the number of credits issued each month to track returns.

Want List: Customers prefer the convenience of one-stop shopping. They expect businesses to maintain the correct inventory in the quantities required for larger sales.

Special Orders: Handling special orders requires a trained individual who understands the logistics involved in procuring unique items, handling freight, and managing any special charges. They should also have a good understanding of the product being ordered.

Large Branch Specialist: Branches with a substantial number of employees, such as 30 or more, should have specialists in place for crucial functions such as inventory processes, shipping processes, and accounts receivable (AR) processes. Everyone needs to be familiar with the branch's processes for receiving, storing, and shipping materials.

Finding the Right People: Continuous interviewing is crucial for finding new people who are eager to learn about the business and contribute to its success.

Correct Number of People: To gauge the adequacy of the workforce, a useful measurement is the monthly gross profit earned by the branch divided by the number of full-time employees (GP\$/FTE). A target number could be exceeding \$10,000 per full-time employee.

Balancing Expenses and Sales: Both expense control and sales growth are essential. With the increase in the number of branches, it has become crucial to closely monitor and control every expense category, especially since the largest expense category is typically people. Budgets and percentages of gross profit calculations provide effective means for expense control.

To-Do List: Despite having everything digitally stored, managers are recommended to take a moment at the end of each day to create a prioritized to-do list for the following day, ensuring tasks from the current day are carried over. This simple practice can significantly enhance productivity.

Low-Margin Sales: There are two types of low-margin sales. The first is a large-volume sale with a low margin, which typically requires discussion among the manager, department head, and salesperson before finalizing the sale. The second type is a low-margin sale with regular quantity, which should raise concerns for regular sales with a margin of less than 25%.

Operations: Managers can derive great value by actively engaging in every operational process. By immersing themselves in the order or process, they gain better insights and can provide effective guidance. Inventory turnover is also important to track, and having 5-6 turns is generally considered acceptable. Another factor to consider with inventory turns is the margin. Some distributors

CHAPTER 8:

STRONG TEAMS: COLLABORATION AND CULTURE

Introduction

In today's competitive business world, working together as a team is more important than having amazing talent. This Chapter will explore how creating a collaborative environment and fostering a positive team culture is critical for success. We will also discuss the challenges of dealing with self-centered and toxic individuals and the importance of screening for certain traits during the hiring process.

The Power of Working Together

Understanding the benefits of collaboration is essential for fostering a thriving team environment. Collaboration goes beyond simply working alongside one another; it involves harnessing the collective intelligence and expertise of team members to achieve common goals. One of the key advantages of collaboration is its role in driving innovation. When individuals from diverse backgrounds and disciplines come together, they bring unique perspectives and ideas to the table, sparking creativity and generating new solutions to challenges.

Moreover, collaboration plays a significant role in problem-solving. By pooling together different viewpoints and skill sets, teams can tackle complex issues from various angles, leading to more comprehensive and effective problem-solving processes. Additionally, the synergy created through collaboration often leads to more informed decision-making. As team members share their insights and engage in constructive discussions, they can reach well-rounded conclusions that consider multiple viewpoints and potential outcomes.

Emphasizing the value of diverse perspectives and skills within a team is crucial. Each team member brings a set of unique strengths and experiences, and when combined, these attributes can lead to better overall results. Collaboration enables individuals to complement one another's abilities, filling gaps and maximizing the team's collective potential.

In conclusion, embracing collaboration as a cornerstone of team dynamics offers numerous benefits, such as fostering innovation, enhancing problem-solving capabilities, and facilitating more informed decision-making. By recognizing the power of working together and valuing the diversity of perspectives and skills within the team, organizations can harness the true potential of their teams and achieve greater success in their endeavors.

Culture and Chemistry as Key Factors

Team culture and chemistry are fundamental aspects that significantly influence the success and effectiveness of a cohesive and high-performing team. A positive and inclusive team culture fosters a sense of belonging and unity among team members, allowing them to work collaboratively and harmoniously towards common objectives. When team members feel valued, supported, and respected, they are more likely to be engaged and motivated, leading to increased productivity and creativity.

Trust, communication, and respect are essential pillars of a strong team culture. Trust forms the foundation upon which team members can rely on one another, enabling them to delegate tasks, share responsibilities, and embrace open feedback. Effective communication ensures that information flows freely, ideas are exchanged, and conflicts are resolved constructively. Respectful interactions create a safe and supportive environment where team members feel comfortable expressing their thoughts and concerns without fear of judgment.

Team-building activities play a crucial role in nurturing team chemistry. Such activities can range from fun and interactive games to challenging problem-solving exercises, all aimed at fostering camaraderie and collaboration. By participating in these activities, team members develop a deeper understanding of one another's strengths and weaknesses, building mutual trust and appreciation.

Open communication is a powerful tool for developing team chemistry. Encouraging regular team meetings, where ideas are shared and discussed openly, promotes a culture of transparency and inclusivity. Setting clear, shared goals helps align team members' efforts and provides a sense of purpose and direction.

In conclusion, team culture and chemistry are pivotal factors that contribute to building a strong and cohesive team. Emphasizing trust, communication, and respect establishes a supportive and productive environment, where team members feel valued and motivated. Team-building activities and shared goals further enhance collaboration and understanding among team members, leading to a team that can overcome challenges and achieve outstanding results.

Overcoming Team Challenges

Self-centered behavior within a team can have a detrimental impact on teamwork and overall performance. When team members prioritize their individual needs over the collective goals, it can lead to conflicts, reduced collaboration, and decreased productivity. To address self-centeredness, it is crucial to promote collective responsibility and empathy among team members. Encouraging a sense of shared ownership for the team's success helps foster a culture where individuals understand that their actions directly influence the overall outcomes.

Creating an environment where team members actively practice empathy can also mitigate self-centeredness. Empathy allows team members to understand and appreciate each other's perspectives, building stronger bonds and promoting mutual support. By acknowledging and respecting the feelings and needs of others, team members can work together more effectively and develop a deeper sense of camaraderie.

Setting clear expectations for teamwork is another essential strategy to combat self-centered behavior. Leaders and managers should communicate the importance of collaboration and outline specific guidelines for how team members should interact and contribute to group efforts. This clarity ensures that everyone is aware of their responsibilities and the collective objectives, reducing the likelihood of individual-focused actions that hinder team progress.

In conclusion, addressing self-centered behavior within a team is vital to fostering a cohesive and high-performing group. By promoting collective responsibility, encouraging empathy, and setting clear teamwork expectations, teams can overcome challenges related to self-centeredness and work together harmoniously towards shared goals.

Handling Toxic Employees

Toxic employees can have detrimental effects on team morale, productivity, and employee retention. Their negative attitudes and behaviors can create a toxic work environment, leading to increased conflicts and reduced overall performance. Recognizing toxic behavior early on is crucial to addressing it proactively. By being attentive to signs of toxicity, such as excessive negativity, lack of teamwork, and disruptive behaviors, managers can intervene before the toxicity spreads further. Implementing performance management processes that focus on addressing toxic behavior and providing constructive feedback can help protect the well-being of the team. Open and honest communication with toxic employees about their behavior and its impact on the team is essential to encourage change. Moreover, fostering a positive and supportive work culture can help prevent toxic behaviors from taking root in the first place, promoting a healthier and more productive team dynamic.

Leadership's Role in Building a Great Team

Leaders play a crucial role in building a great team by shaping its culture, fostering engagement, and driving performance. They set a positive example through their actions and attitudes, demonstrating the values and behaviors they expect from their team. Effective leaders encourage collaboration among team members, recognizing the power of diverse perspectives and collective efforts. They inspire team members to excel and reach their full potential, providing support and guidance to help them grow. By creating a motivating and supportive environment, leaders empower their teams to achieve exceptional results and foster a culture of continuous improvement.

Developing Effective Leadership Skills

1. Develop Effective Communication Skills:

    - Encourage open and honest communication among team members.

    - Provide training on active listening and effective verbal and written communication.

    - Foster a culture where feedback is welcomed and constructively delivered.

2. Enhance Emotional Intelligence:

    - Promote self-awareness and understanding of emotions.

    - Provide resources for developing empathy and emotional regulation.

    - Encourage leaders to recognize and consider the emotions of team members.

3. Cultivate Coaching Abilities:

- Provide training on coaching techniques and mentoring skills.

- Encourage leaders to identify and nurture individual strengths in team members.

- Support a coaching culture that values continuous learning and growth.

4. Emphasize Ongoing Leadership Development:

- Support leaders in attending leadership development programs and workshops.

- Encourage leaders to seek regular feedback and self-assessment.

- Create individualized leadership development plans for continuous improvement.

5. Foster a Culture of Continuous Improvement:

- Encourage leaders to lead by example in embracing continuous improvement.

- Implement regular team assessments and feedback sessions.

- Recognize and celebrate efforts to suggest and implement process improvements.

By following these concise instructions, leaders can develop crucial skills that contribute to team excellence and create a culture of continuous improvement within the organization.

Screening for Cultural Fit and Identifying Narcissistic Traits

In the hiring process, it's crucial to make sure new employees fit well with the company's values and how the team works together. This helps create a strong and cooperative work environment. When people fit in, they can adapt quickly, get along with others, and boost productivity and morale.

To find the right fit, hiring managers can use some strategies. Firstly, they need to clearly define the company's core values and mission to see if candidates share similar beliefs. During interviews, asking questions about past experiences can show if candidates' responses match the company's values.

Also, it's essential to see how candidates interact with the team. Group discussions or team activities can reveal how well candidates work together and communicate. Observing how they fit into the company's work environment and get along with potential colleagues gives valuable information about their cultural fit.

Remember, cultural fit doesn't mean looking for identical people. It's about finding individuals who share the company's values and can collaborate with the existing team. By checking for cultural fit, companies can build a strong team that works well together and leads the company to success.

Recognizing and Managing Narcissistic Traits

Dealing with people who have narcissistic traits can be challenging, especially in a team environment. Such individuals often prioritize their own needs and seek constant admiration, which can lead to conflicts and disrupt team harmony. Managers need to recognize and address these traits to maintain a positive and productive team dynamic.

During the hiring process, it's crucial to screen for narcissism to avoid potential issues later on. This can be achieved by paying attention to certain behaviors and attitudes exhibited by candidates during interviews. Look for signs of excessive self-importance, a lack of empathy, and a strong desire for recognition or praise. By being mindful of these traits, managers can make more informed decisions when selecting new team members.

If a narcissistic individual is already part of the team, it's important to manage their behavior effectively. One strategy is to set clear boundaries and expectations for teamwork and collaboration. Encourage open communication and ensure that everyone's contributions are valued equally. Additionally, providing constructive feedback and highlighting the importance of working together as a team can help address any narcissistic tendencies.

It's also crucial to foster a positive and supportive team culture where everyone's strengths and ideas are appreciated. By promoting a culture of mutual respect and cooperation, managers can create an environment where narcissistic traits are less likely to thrive. Overall, recognizing and managing narcissistic traits is essential for maintaining a cohesive and successful team.

Conclusion:

Creating a collaborative work environment and fostering a positive team culture is crucial for the success of Coburn Supply Company. By working together, addressing self-centeredness and toxicity, and developing effective leadership skills, managers can build a strong and high-performing team. It is also important to screen candidates for cultural fit and be aware of narcissistic traits during the hiring process. These efforts will contribute to creating a collaborative and successful team at Coburn Supply Company.

CHAPTER 9:

INSPIRING LEADERSHIP: THE LEGACY OF MR. JAMES MALONEY

In the journey of creating a thriving business, effective leadership plays a pivotal role. This Chapter pays tribute to Mr. James Maloney, a remarkable mentor who inspired countless individuals at Coburn Supply Company. His valuable teachings and profound impact on the company have shaped the principles and values outlined in this book.

A Balanced Approach

Mr. Maloney had a conservative approach to business operations. He always ensured stability and financial prudence. When it came to helping people, he demonstrated a compassionate and supportive nature. Mr. Maloney was very conservative when it came to business but very giving when it came to helping people.

Customer-Centric Focus

Mr. Maloney had an unwavering commitment to providing exceptional customer service. Emphasizing the importance of the "WANT LIST" and its role in ensuring product availability for customers. He was known for his meticulous attention to detail in managing accounts receivable, understanding the importance of timely payments, and building strong relationships with customers.

Managing Risk and Credit was also very important to Mr. Maloney and establishing the culture early on in the business. He was big on the role of Coburn Supply as a middleman between factories and customers, taking on the risk of providing credit to those contractors and customers. He knew that we needed to sometimes finance those customers and manage that credit to keep them and Coburns in business. He took time to know the customers and provided those with integrity and honesty with larger lines of credit. The only reason we are in business is because the factory knows that we extend credit to promote their products. We have to stay in constant communication with our customers to effectively manage these receivables. Part of our success over the years is because we know how to analyze credit extended to our contractor customers. We have to know this well and as a company, we are very experienced. Most banks would not loan these small businesses and contractors the amount of credit that they need. If all contractors paid their bills every month, the factories would "go around us" and sell to them directly. The fact that we manage this credit and risk for the factories creates our position in the industry. Mr. Maloney understood that maintaining a trustworthy customer base was essential for sustainable growth.

Mr. Maloney had a keen ability to read faces and identify the emotions of people. This skill set is something that managers should strive to develop. "You have to be approachable" Mr. Maloney always said, to customers and employees. "The customer and employees need to be able to come to you with whatever problem they have. Always be approachable." Mr. Maloney's leadership and profound impact on Coburn Supply Company serves as an enduring inspiration for us all. As we navigate the ever-changing business landscape, let us carry forward his teachings and principles to build a prosperous future for our organization.

Conclusion

We emphasize the importance of measurement and evaluation. We believe in measuring every aspect of our operations to identify areas for improvement and optimize performance. By setting clear objectives and regularly evaluating our employees' performance, we can ensure accountability and drive success. Controlling expenses and balancing expense control with revenue growth is critical for effective management. Efficient operations, accuracy, and efficiency are key to maintaining profitability and delivering value to our customers.

In the realm of operations, we prioritize smooth and efficient processes. From order fulfillment to inventory management, we strive for accuracy, timely delivery, and customer satisfaction. By optimizing inventory turnover, managing credits effectively, and offering a diverse range of products, we enhance our operations and meet the needs of our customers. Tracking dead stock, managing special orders and returns, and measuring performance provide valuable insights for continuous improvement. We value employee motivation, clear communication, and development, as they contribute to a high-performing team that drives our operational success.

When we align the sales, management, and operations cultures, we create a cohesive and effective organization. By fostering a culture of collaboration, communication, and continuous improvement, we can achieve our goals and thrive in a rapidly evolving business landscape. Let us embrace these cultures and work together to shape a successful future for our organization.

ABOUT THE AUTHOR

Alfred "Trey" Berlin III, the author of this book, brings a wealth of knowledge and experience to the table, garnered from over 50 years in the distribution business. With a humble dedication to managing and building stores for Coburn Supply Company, Trey has made a lasting impact on the industry. His commitment to mentorship and carrying on the legacy of Mr. James Maloney has been his mission throughout his career.

His hands-on experience and natural leadership abilities have allowed him to navigate industry complexities with remarkable success. He recognizes the value of sharing knowledge and empowering others. In this book, Trey Berlin shares his collection of notes and lessons, providing readers with unique insights from various positions on the distribution team. From practical store management strategies to lessons on building large-scale growth, this book is designed to help young professionals accelerate their careers in distribution.